THE COMPASSIONATE ICE AGENT

PAST, PRESENT, AND FUTURE

A MESSAGE FROM

DR. ABRAHAM KHOUREIS, Ph.D.
The Apostle of Compassionate Leadership

COPYRIGHT NOTICE

ANG POWER PUBLISHING HOUSE
ANGPowerPHouse@Gmail.com
ISBN: 978-1-966837-46-6

Disclaimer: The author and publisher have made every effort to ensure the accuracy of the information in this publication. However, they assume no responsibility for errors or omissions or for any consequences resulting from the use of the information provided. This book is intended for educational and informational purposes only and does not constitute professional or legal advice.

Printed in the United States of America

TABLE OF CONTENTS

This page intentionally left blank for your reading reflection

Note & Disclaimer

This book is a work of literature inspired by true events. While it draws from present and historical accounts, traditions, and collective memory, certain characters, dialogues, and scenes have been adapted for narrative purposes. Although it is based on accurate resources, it is not intended to serve as a definitive historical record.

Any resemblance to actual persons, living or deceased, as well as to organizations, institutions, governments, or groups, beyond the well-known historical figures and entities referenced, is entirely coincidental and unintentional.

This work is not affiliated with, endorsed by, or representative of the policies, practices, or official positions of U.S. Immigration and Customs Enforcement, the Department of Homeland Security, or any government agency. It reflects the author's perspectives and is intended solely for discussion, reflection, and educational insight into compassionate leadership within enforcement settings. Images are artistic representations and do not imply endorsement by any individual, entity, or estate.

The purpose of this work is to honor the essence of events and to explore their moral, spiritual, and human significance through the medium of authentic and real storytelling.

Preface

Personally, I believe in the American experience. Not necessarily the political idea of America, not the slogans, not the arguments on television, but the lived experience that millions feel in their bones the first moment they step onto this soil. America at its best is dignity. It is fairness. It is the home of second chances. It is the belief that a human being's worth is not erased by their birthplace or their circumstances.

The American experience belongs to everyone who lives under its sky, the original inhabitants of the land, the settlers, the native-born, the immigrant, the settled and the newly arrived.

But there are moments when that promise cracks. Moments when the America many people knew and carry in their hearts suddenly feels distant, almost unrecognizable.

One afternoon in Los Angeles, an older woman stood behind her fruit stand. She was small, no taller than five feet. Her hands were busy with the simple work of the day, arranging fruit, speaking softly to customers, living the quiet life of someone trying to survive.

Then ICE agents approached.

The moment she saw them, fear took over her entire body. She ran. Not the run of someone avoiding a ticket or a fine. It was the run of someone who believed danger had arrived. She stumbled as she tried to escape. Her steps were uneven, desperate, almost childlike in their panic.

She was stopped a short distance away. Placed face down on the pavement. Her small frame pressed against the ground. Her body shaking. Her voice breaking into cries that did not need translation. Fear has one language. It sounds the same in every language, every tongue, and every country.

That scene did not belong to the America I and many believe in. It felt like something from a more primitive place, a place before law learned to walk with dignity. A place where fear leads and humanity struggles to keep up.

The agents had authority. No one can deny that. But authority alone does not define a nation. The atmosphere around that woman lacked humanity. It lacked compassion. And in that moment, the country built on dignity felt as if it had forgotten its own reflection.

That older woman was not alone. Similar scenes appear again and again. Men trembling as if their existence itself were a crime. Mothers hiding their children not because they committed wrongdoing, but because they feared humiliation. Families treated as threats instead of human beings trying to breathe through another day.

When fear strips away compassion, the American experience becomes tarnished. Not only for those who are chased, but for those who wear the uniform as well. Something inside the nation grows colder. Something inside the people grows harder.

America was never meant to be only about enforcement. It is more than borders. More than policies drafted in offices far removed from the lives they shape. America is a human experience. It is the feeling of fairness. The belief that dignity does not depend on paperwork.

Those who live here without legal permission have still tasted that promise. They have seen neighbors help each other. They have worked hard and built lives from nothing. They have believed, sometimes more than the native-born, that this country offers a chance to rise.

When dignity is denied to them, especially in their most vulnerable moments, the betrayal is not only theirs. It is the nation's. It is a stain on the idea that America stands for something higher than fear.

Most undocumented people do not come here for chaos. They come because they heard about a place where effort matters. Where the door is not permanently closed. Where life can begin again. When that door closes in humiliation, the shame does not follow them back across the border. It stays here. It lingers in the culture, in the institutions, in the conscience of the nation.

Enforcement without dignity becomes cruelty. And cruelty has never been the strength of America. Compassion has. When compassion disappears, the damage is visible everywhere. It appears in the streets. It appears in the tired eyes of agents carrying the emotional weight of their duties. It appears in families separated without even a moment of respect to soften the pain. It appears in the slow hardening of a nation that once prided itself on fairness.

Strength and compassion are not enemies. They were always meant to walk side by side. The strongest nations in history were not the cruelest ones. They were the ones that knew how to combine power with conscience.

The American experience should remain unbroken. It should remain a light. Enforcement should reflect the values that built this country. Agents should feel proud not only of their authority, but of their humanity. Those who must leave should carry with them the memory that they were treated fairly, even in sorrow.

America is at its best when it remembers that every human being carries dignity. When compassion guides strength, everyone stands taller. The agent stands taller. The community stands taller. The nation stands taller.

This book is a reminder that better choices are always possible. A call to agents, leaders, and the country itself to rise to the level of its values.

As we begin, let's pray, May America never forget who it is. May it never forget who it must continue becoming. And may its leaders be guided by compassion in their hearts and wisdom in their minds.

To Every ICE Agent

You stand at one of the hardest intersections in public service, where law meets human suffering and where your decisions shape more than procedure, they shape lives. The purpose of this book is to remind you of the power you hold and the humanity you must never lose.

Compassion is not weakness. Compassion is clarity. It sharpens your judgment. It steadies your mind. It protects your moral center. And it ensures that you do not carry the weight of unnecessary harm long after your shift ends.

You chose this path for reasons you may or may not share with others. But whatever brought you to serve our country, you are not defined by policy alone. You are defined by how you carry out that policy. By the choices you make in moments that no one else witnesses. By the dignity you give or refuse to give. By the person you remain, or the person you abandon, in the face of pressure, fear, or exhaustion.

This book is a reminder of your past, a reflection of

your present, and an invitation for your future.

It is your reminder to becoming a compassionate ICE agent, not a softer agent, not a weaker agent, but a wiser, steadier, clearer, and more human one.

Your job asks for authority. Your humanity asks for compassion. The true compassionate agent carries both.

Introduction

This book is written for the agents who carry out some of the most difficult responsibilities in immigration enforcement, and for the leaders who guide them. It is written for those who stand at the center of one of the most emotionally charged and politically debated areas of American life. But above all, it is written for the conscience of a nation that must never lose sight of its humanity or its promise.

Immigration enforcement is not just a profession. It is a daily encounter with fear, hope, desperation, and uncertainty. It places human vulnerability face to face with human authority. It tests the moral strength of the agents involved and the ethical clarity of the system that sends them into the field. When carried out with discipline and compassion, it protects the nation. When carried out without humanity, it harms everyone involved, including the agents themselves.

I am offering this book as a reminder, and it is offered with gratitude. It thanks agents for their dedication and service to the country, and it reminds agents of their humanity and of the American promise they represent. It recognizes the dedication required to serve in a role that is often misunderstood, criticized, and emotionally draining. Behind every uniform is a person who carries long hours, difficult encounters, and the quiet burdens that follow them home at the end of the day.

Many agents are tired. Many families carry the emotional strain of this work. Many agents try to act with compassion even when the systems around them are built for speed rather than dignity. Many feel caught between duty and conscience. Many simply need leadership that reminds them that compassion is not a liability. It is a strength.

The purpose here is not to change the law. The law is the framework within which the nation operates. The deeper question is how that law is carried out?

Compassion does not weaken enforcement. It refines it. It steadies it. It makes it more effective, more controlled, and more reflective of the values America claims as its foundation. Compassion does not replace discipline. Compassion strengthens discipline. It keeps decisions grounded in clarity and dignity rather than frustration or haste.

The lessons in these pages come from observation, experience, and a deep belief that the American experience is worth protecting. There have been moments when compassion transformed a tense situation into a respectful one. There have also been moments when the absence of compassion turned a simple encounter into lasting trauma. Those moments shaped the need for this book. They guided its tone and its purpose. This work is not written as criticism. It is written as protection of the American experience.

America was built by people searching for safety, opportunity, and dignity. Those values should not disappear when the law must be enforced. They should become more visible. The undocumented who arrive here have seen the best of this country.

They have received kindness from neighbors, mercy from strangers, and hope from opportunities that did not exist in their homelands. When their journeys end, they should not walk away believing cruelty defines this nation. They should leave knowing that even in sorrow, America treated them with dignity.

Agents deserve guidance that helps them preserve

their humanity. Leaders deserve a vision that helps them elevate their teams. Migrants deserve respect, even when the outcome is difficult. And the nation deserves an immigration system that does not betray its moral identity.

This is my invitation to elevate enforcement into a higher form of leadership: Compassion. It is a reminder that strength without compassion becomes domination, while strength with compassion becomes justice. It calls for enforcement aligned with dignity. It calls for the protection of the conscience of every agent who serves under the weight of national authority.

The American experience belongs to all who touch it. The responsibility is not only to uphold the law, but to uphold the humanity that gives the law meaning.

The hope behind these pages is simple. Agents should feel seen, respected, and guided. Migrants should feel acknowledged, understood, and honored. Leaders should feel the weight of their influence and the responsibility of their example.

America's greatness has always depended on compassion. Let that compassion remain at the center of enforcement. Let the American experience remain worthy of its name.

This page intentionally left blank for your reading reflection

Chapter One:
The Weight Ice Agents Carry

Every ICE agent knows that behind the badge there is a responsibility that follows them long after the shift ends. The public sees the uniform, the vehicle, and the authority, but rarely do they understand the emotional weight agents carry. The job demands discipline, vigilance, and constant awareness. It exposes agents to fear, desperation, and human suffering in ways most people never witness. Over time, this has a cost. It shapes the mind, hardens the body, and challenges the heart.

Agents step into homes where children cry because they do not understand why their parent is being taken away. They face individuals who do not resist, not because they accept their fate, but because exhaustion has replaced hope. They speak to people who traveled thousands of miles to escape violence, only to find themselves facing another form of fear. They make decisions in moments where no choice feels right. These encounters remain long after the operation is over. They follow agents into their cars, their homes, their families, and their sleep.

This book acknowledges that weight. It respects the emotional toll the job takes on the men and women who serve. Many agents entered their roles believing they were defending the country, upholding the law, and protecting national security. And they are. But they are also human beings, and human beings absorb what they see. No training fully prepares them for the emotional complexity of enforcing laws on people who are often frightened, poor, or desperate. No manual warns them that compassion and concern, when ignored too long, can turn into quiet emotional harm.

Compassion is not only a gift agents offer others. It is something they must offer themselves. When agents allow compassion into their work, they protect their own mental health. Compassion reminds them that their authority is not meant to crush dignity but to uphold it. Compassion anchors them, helping them carry out their duties without losing the better parts of themselves.

Every agent deserves to serve with a clear conscience. Every agent deserves to feel that their work strengthens the nation rather than harms it. And every agent deserves leadership that recognizes the emotional realities of this profession. By embracing compassion, agents do not weaken the mission. They strengthen it. They give the uniform meaning. They protect the integrity of the badge. And they protect their own humanity while carrying out the most difficult parts of this job.

Chapter Two: The Benefits of Practicing Compassion

Compassion is not something extra you add to your work. It is a skill that strengthens every part of your performance. Many agents think compassion creates softness or hesitation. In truth, compassion creates clarity. It makes you sharper, more aware, and more effective. When you practice compassion, you elevate the quality of your decisions and the way you engage with the people in front of you.

One of the first benefits is emotional control. Compassion teaches you to respond instead of react. It slows down the impulse to meet tension with more tension. It allows you to stay steady when someone is afraid, confused, or angry. This steadiness protects you. It keeps your mind open and your judgment clear.

Compassion also improves communication. When you speak to people with respect, you get more cooperation. People understand you better. They listen more closely. They follow instructions with less resistance. Even if they disagree with what is happening, your tone can reduce fear and prevent unnecessary escalation. A compassionate voice calms the room, and a calm room keeps everyone safer.

Another benefit is the protection of your own mental health. The work you do exposes you to hardship and conflict on a regular basis. Without compassion, you begin to harden yourself to survive the emotional weight. That hardening works in the moment, but over time it changes you. It distances you from your family. It shortens your patience. It makes sleep more difficult. It follows you home.

Compassion prevents that erosion. It keeps your humanity active. It gives you a way to release the emotional pressure instead of carrying it around. You feel more balanced, more present, and more alive. You become the version of yourself your loved ones recognize. This job demands strength, but compassion gives you a strength that does not crack under pressure.

Compassion improves your safety as well. It helps you read people more accurately. When you see a person as a human being rather than a task, you notice details you would otherwise miss. You interpret body language better. You understand the difference between fear and aggression. You separate confusion from defiance. This awareness helps you prevent conflict before it begins.

Compassion also strengthens your professionalism. It reminds you that authority is not about dominance. It is about responsibility. When you speak with dignity and act with fairness, you uphold the values the badge represents. You become a model for other agents. You influence the culture around you. And you build a reputation that earns trust from colleagues and supervisors.

Compassion makes your legacy cleaner. One day, the uniform will come off. When that day arrives, you will not measure your career by how many people you processed. You will measure it by how you carried your authority. You will ask yourself whether you acted with the integrity you believe in. You will remember the moments when compassion made you proud of who you were.

Compassion protects your identity, your family, your integrity, and your future. It transforms the way you work and the way you see yourself. In a profession that can easily consume your humanity, compassion is the anchor that keeps you grounded.

This page intentionally left blank for your reading reflection

Chapter Three:

The Cost of Losing Compassion

Compassion does not vanish all at once. It fades slowly, day by day, assignment by assignment, shift by shift. And when it begins to fade, the job starts to reshape you in ways that you notice only after the changes settle in. This erosion affects your behavior, your judgment, and ultimately your sense of self.

When compassion weakens, impatience rises. You find yourself reacting from irritation rather than clarity. You speak faster, not because the situation demands it, but because your patience is stretched thin. You stop explaining things that would calm the room. You expect people to understand your instructions even when fear or language barriers make that impossible. This impatience increases tension, not because the job requires it, but because compassion is no longer guiding your responses.

Without compassion, the work becomes emotionally heavier. You begin carrying frustration with you long after the interaction ends. Small situations feel bigger. Simple misunderstandings turn into conflicts. You start to dread certain assignments. You avoid eye contact with the people you process because you do not want to feel anything. But feeling nothing is not strength. It is a sign of emotional fatigue.

Losing compassion also affects your relationships. You bring home silence, irritability, and emotional distance. Your family feels something is wrong even when you tell them everything is fine. You react quickly to minor frustrations. Your patience shortens with the people you love most. This is the invisible cost of compassion fading inside you.

The job begins to take more from you than it gives. You lose sleep. You replay moments in your head. You feel unsettled without knowing why. You become guarded, even around people who mean no harm. You begin to move through life as if everything is a potential threat. This is not who you are. This is what happens when compassion is pushed aside for too long.

There is a deeper cost as well. Moral injury. Moral injury occurs when you act in ways that conflict with your values or witness things that trouble your conscience. You may not speak about it, but you feel it. You feel it in your chest. You feel it in moments of stillness. You feel it when you look in the mirror and remember the person you once were.

Compassion is not a weakness. It is protection. It keeps you aligned with your values. It keeps you whole. It shields your identity from the distortions of prolonged stress. Without compassion, the job becomes a constant battle with yourself.

Choosing compassion is choosing self-preservation. It is choosing mental clarity. It is choosing the version of yourself that you still want to recognize years from now.

The job also becomes heavier without compassion. Stress accumulates. You become tired in ways that rest cannot fix. The work begins to feel like a burden instead of a purpose. You wake up already tense. You drive to work already guarded. You lose the sense of meaning that once guided your decisions. Compassion is what gives purpose to duty. Without it, duty becomes weight.

Compassion is not just for those you encounter. It is for you. It is the shield that keeps the job from shaping you into someone you never meant to be. When compassion leaves, the job becomes harder. Your relationships suffer. Your inner peace fades.

Your identity weakens. Recognizing these costs is not criticism. It is the first step back to becoming the person you chose to be.

Chapter Four:
Compassion as Strength

Compassion is often misunderstood as softness, but the truth is the opposite. Compassion requires strength. It requires discipline. It requires self-control. It requires awareness. When you practice compassion, you demonstrate the highest level of professional maturity. You show that you can manage your emotions, understand your environment, and guide situations with clarity rather than force.

Compassion strengthens judgment. It helps you see beyond the surface of a situation. You recognize fear, not as defiance but as fear. You see confusion, not as resistance but as confusion. You understand that people in distress rarely communicate perfectly. Compassion brings insight. Insight leads to better decisions. Better decisions lead to safer outcomes.

Compassion strengthens presence. It keeps you calm when others are losing control. It prevents you from escalating situations unintentionally. It allows you to respond with authority rather than aggression. It reminds you that your tone, your posture, and your choices influence the entire environment. When you lead with compassion, you set the tone for everyone in the room.

Compassion strengthens internal discipline. It keeps your pride in check. It prevents your ego from interfering with your professionalism. It brings humility, which is essential in a position of power. When you approach people with compassion, you protect your integrity. You ensure that your authority is used responsibly.

Compassion strengthens the connection between mind and heart. It keeps you human in a job that can sometimes feel mechanical. It allows you to see the dignity in each person, even when the situation is tense. Compassion does not weaken your authority. It deepens it. People respond more positively to an agent who is firm but fair, structured but respectful, authoritative but humane.

Compassion strengthens your legacy. Years from now, you will not remember every name or every file, but you will remember the moments when compassion guided you. You will remember the times when you acted in alignment with your values. You will remember the satisfaction of knowing that you were a strong agent and a good human being at the same time.

True strength is not loud. It is not forceful. It is not aggressive. True strength is quiet, intentional, and rooted in emotional discipline. Compassion is a form of strength because it requires you to stay centered even when the environment around you is unstable.

Compassion demands self-control. Anyone can react with anger. Anyone can raise their voice. Anyone can lose patience. But staying steady when someone else is losing control requires maturity. Remaining calm when someone is afraid requires awareness. Choosing dignity over dominance requires discipline. This is strength, and not everyone has it.

Compassion sharpens decision-making. When you see the human being in front of you, you interpret behavior accurately. You recognize when someone is overwhelmed rather than resisting. You understand when someone is trying to cooperate but lacks the words. You read fear instead of confusing it with defiance. Compassion gives you insight. Insight leads to better, safer decisions.

Compassion deepens your authority. When people sense fairness in you, they follow your instructions more readily. They trust your leadership. They see you as someone in power, not someone abusing power. Authority gained through respect lasts longer than authority gained through intimidation.

Compassion strengthens your professionalism. It prevents ego from influencing your behavior. It keeps your pride in check. It ensures that your actions represent the best of what enforcement can be. It prevents you from acting out of frustration or exhaustion. Compassion is professional discipline in action.

Compassion also sustains you. It allows you to carry your responsibilities without emotional collapse. It prevents burnout. It protects your moral center. It gives you the strength to keep showing up with clarity and purpose. Hardness collapses over time. Compassion endures.

There is nothing weak about compassion. It is courage. It is leadership. It is the foundation of honorable service.

Chapter Five:

How Compassion Improves Every Encounter

Every encounter begins before a single word is spoken. It begins the moment an agent steps into a space. People sense presence before they hear instructions. They read posture, tone, and energy. They look for signs of danger or safety. Compassion, when carried into that first moment, quietly transforms the entire interaction.

A calm presence changes the atmosphere. Shoulders lower. Voices soften. People become more cooperative. They listen more carefully. They ask fewer frantic questions. They feel less threatened. Even when the news delivered is difficult, compassion softens the emotional impact. The outcome of the encounter may not change, but the experience of it does.

Tone is one of the most powerful tools an agent carries. A steady voice communicates control and safety. A harsh voice creates confusion and fear. People respond to the emotional rhythm set by the agent in front of them. When tone carries compassion, it creates a structure for the entire interaction. It tells the room that authority is present, but it is not there to humiliate or frighten. It is there to carry out the law with order and dignity.

Patience is another quiet form of strength. Rushing people increases fear. Fear leads to resistance. Resistance leads to conflict. When a person is given a moment to breathe, to process, or to steady themselves, cooperation often follows. This does not slow the operation. It reduces disruption. Compassion is not inefficient. Conflict is what wastes time. Compassion, when practiced with discipline, becomes the more efficient path.

Clarity is also a form of compassion. People fear what they do not understand. A brief, calm explanation of what is happening can remove layers of anxiety. Simple words, spoken steadily, reduce panic. They reduce misunderstandings. They prevent unnecessary emotional escalation. Clarity allows people to face a difficult moment with some sense of order rather than chaos.

Compassion also improves safety. When people feel respected, they are less likely to act unpredictably. They are less likely to challenge authority or lash out in fear. Respect lowers emotional intensity. It gives the encounter a structure that feels controlled rather than explosive. In this way, compassion becomes a form of protection, not only for the people involved, but for the agents themselves.

In the field, leadership is not always defined by rank. It is often defined by presence. An agent who carries calm and compassion influences the entire team. Others adjust their tone. Movements become more measured. Conversations become more controlled. One steady presence can shape the pace of the entire operation. Compassion, in that sense, becomes leadership expressed through conduct.

Compassion also shapes the agent's inner experience. Encounters handled with dignity leave fewer emotional scars. The end of the shift feels lighter. Sleep comes more easily. Conversations at home carry less tension. A clear conscience is not a small thing. It is one of the greatest protections an agent can carry through a long career.

Every encounter is shaped by the energy an agent brings into it. The tone, the environment, and the emotional temperature of the moment are influenced

long before the first instruction is given. Compassion turns encounters into manageable moments rather than escalating conflicts.

A steady tone signals control. It tells people that the situation is being guided, not inflamed. When tone carries fairness, people are more likely to listen and comply. They sense professionalism rather than hostility. Tone matters more than many realize, and compassion shapes that tone.

Patience creates space for cooperation. Fear causes people to freeze, panic, or resist. Patience breaks through that fear. It shows confidence, not weakness. It allows the agent to control the emotional rhythm of the encounter. With patience, there are fewer misunderstandings and fewer unnecessary escalations.

Clarity brings understanding. When people know what to expect, panic fades. Simple explanations reduce uncertainty. They give people the dignity of understanding what is happening to them. That dignity often leads to smoother, more organized interactions.

Restraint builds trust. Not every situation requires the full display of authority. Sometimes direction is enough. When authority is used with restraint, it signals professionalism. It shows that the power of the badge is understood and carried responsibly. That kind of authority earns respect rather than fear.

In chaotic moments, compassion becomes an anchor. When tension rises, a steady presence restores balance. When confusion grows, clear words restore order. People naturally gravitate toward the person who feels most stable. Compassion provides that stability.

Encounters guided by compassion tend to be cleaner, safer, and more productive. They carry less conflict, less confusion, and fewer emotional wounds. The law is still enforced. The mission is still carried out. But the process reflects dignity rather than fear.

Compassion does not change the authority of the badge. It changes the way that authority is experienced. And in that difference, both the agent and the nation stand taller.

This page intentionally left blank for your reading reflection

Chapter Six: Authority with Dignity

Authority is part of the role. It comes with the badge, the uniform, and the law behind it. But authority alone does not define the quality of the work. Dignity does. Authority used without dignity becomes harshness. Authority carried with dignity becomes leadership. People may not welcome the decisions being made, but they will remember the manner in which those decisions were carried out. When dignity guides the action, respect often follows, even in difficult moments.

Dignity begins with the way an agent speaks. Respectful language opens the door to cooperation. Disrespectful language closes it quickly. Instructions can be firm without being demeaning. A calm voice can carry authority just as effectively as a harsh one. The badge provides the legal power. Character provides the dignity behind it. The two must travel together.

Posture also communicates intention. People read

body language faster than they process words. A calm, balanced posture signals control and professionalism. An aggressive posture signals threat. When posture carries dignity, tension lowers. The situation feels guided rather than dominated. Professional presence does not require intimidation. It requires steadiness.

Restraint is another expression of dignity. Authority means having power, but power does not need to be displayed at its highest level in every situation. Restraint shows discipline. It shows maturity. It reflects self-control. It communicates that authority is not a tool for dominance, but a responsibility to guide the situation with clarity. True authority does not need to overpower. It needs to direct.

Within a unit, dignity influences culture. When one agent consistently acts with respect and professionalism, others notice. Tone shifts. Interactions become more measured. A single example can shape the atmosphere of an entire team. Dignity spreads quietly, through conduct rather than instruction. It builds an environment where professionalism becomes the norm rather than the exception.

Dignity also protects the agent. Actions taken without dignity often return later as regret. Words spoken in frustration tend to echo in the mind long after the moment has passed. When dignity guides behavior, there is less second-guessing. There is less discomfort at the end of the shift. A clear conscience becomes one of the most valuable protections an agent can carry through a long career.

Authority is a tool. Dignity is the manner in which that tool is used. When the two move together, enforcement becomes honorable. Without dignity, authority turns harsh, and harshness leaves damage behind, in the community, in the institution, and in the heart of the person wearing the badge.

Dignity begins with presence. The way an agent stands, the distance kept, the steadiness of movement, all communicate intention. A balanced presence signals confidence. A threatening posture signals insecurity or aggression. When presence carries dignity, the entire interaction rises to a more professional level.

Language follows presence. Words can humiliate or they can guide. Language that mocks, belittles, or dismisses creates resentment and fear. Language that explains, instructs, and respects preserves dignity. The words chosen in the field become a reflection not only of the badge, but of the person wearing it.

Restraint remains one of the clearest signs of dignity. Power does not require constant display. Restraint shows that authority is understood as responsibility. It shows the ability to distinguish between necessary force and unnecessary pressure. That distinction is the mark of professionalism.

Over time, dignity builds credibility. Agents who consistently act with fairness and respect become trusted voices. Supervisors rely on them. Colleagues follow their lead. Even those being processed recognize dignity when they see it. Trust grows, not from authority alone, but from the way authority is carried.

Most importantly, dignity protects the inner life of the agent. Actions guided by dignity leave fewer emotional wounds. There is less regret, fewer restless thoughts, and a stronger sense of alignment between duty and conscience. Dignity keeps the person intact behind the uniform.

Authority without dignity becomes destructive. Authority with dignity becomes leadership. And in the long run, leadership is what gives the badge its true meaning.

This page intentionally left blank for your reading reflection

Chapter Seven: Protecting Your Humanity

Your humanity is your greatest asset. It is what allows you to read situations accurately, communicate effectively, and maintain control with wisdom. But your humanity is also vulnerable in this line of work. The emotional weight of repeated conflict, tension, and difficult stories can erode your sense of self if you do not protect it intentionally.

Protecting your humanity begins with awareness. Recognizing when you are becoming hardened or impatient is the first step. Notice when your tone sharpens unnecessarily. Notice when you detach from your feelings for too long. Notice when stress begins to shape your behavior.

Protecting your humanity requires boundaries. Not everything you see should follow you home. Reflection is healthy. Carrying the emotional pain of others is not. Learn to release what is not yours to hold. You can acknowledge difficulty without letting it define you.

Protecting your humanity means staying connected to your values. Remember why you chose to serve. Remember the standards you set for yourself. Remember the person you want to be in every environment. Values keep you centered. They prevent the job from reshaping you into someone you do not recognize.

Protecting your humanity strengthens your family life. When you show up at home with presence, gentleness, and patience, your relationships deepen. Your family feels you. They know when you are emotionally available. Compassion at work keeps your heart soft enough to connect with them.

Protecting your humanity prevents long-term burnout. The more you harden yourself, the faster exhaustion grows. Compassion keeps your inner world alive. It prevents emotional numbness. It allows you to rest deeply and return to work with clarity.

Your humanity is not a weakness. It is the compass you rely on when the job becomes difficult. Guard it. Honor it. Protect it.

Protecting Your Humanity: Your humanity is not something you leave at home. It is not something you suppress for the sake of professionalism. Your humanity is the instrument through which you interpret the world. It is your compass. It is your strength. But in this line of work, your humanity is constantly tested.

Protecting your humanity requires self-awareness. You must recognize when stress is shaping your responses. You must recognize when your tone sharpens too quickly. You must recognize when you begin to disconnect emotionally. These signs are not failures. They are warnings. They tell you that your inner resources need attention.

It requires emotional boundaries. This does not mean shutting down empathy. It means separating what you can influence from what you cannot. You can enforce the law. You cannot solve every tragedy. You can speak with dignity. You cannot change someone's past. You can treat someone fairly. You cannot control how they interpret the moment. Healthy boundaries allow you to care without breaking.

Protecting your humanity requires connection to your values. You must remember why you chose this profession. You must remember the principles you promised yourself you would never lose. You must remember the version of yourself you want to be. Values keep your identity steady. They guard your sense of purpose.

Protecting your humanity strengthens your life outside of work. When you carry compassion into your home, your relationships stay alive. You stay emotionally open. You show love with clarity. You speak with gentleness. Your family feels your presence instead of your fatigue.

Protecting your humanity prevents burnout. Hardness cracks over time. Compassion absorbs shock. Hardness isolates you. Compassion reconnects you. Hardness makes you brittle. Compassion makes you resilient. Your humanity is not a distraction from your duty. It is the foundation that allows you to perform your duty with integrity.

Chapter Eight:
From Compliance to Character

Following orders is part of your job, but character shapes how you follow them. Compliance without character becomes mechanical and sometimes harmful. Character gives meaning to compliance. It allows you to carry out your duties without losing your moral center.

Character is shown in your tone, your patience, and your restraint. It is shown in your ability to treat people with respect even when you disagree with their choices. It is shown in your capacity to remain calm under pressure. It is shown in your willingness to see the person, not just the policy.

Character is revealed in small decisions, not just major ones. It shows up in the way you say good morning to a colleague. It shows up in the way you speak to someone who does not understand what is happening. It shows up in your reactions when someone is afraid or angry. These moments define the quality of your leadership.

Character protects your integrity. It prevents you from crossing lines that damage your conscience. It helps you stand firm when the environment pushes you toward impatience or detachment. It reminds you that authority is a responsibility, not a right.

Character builds credibility. People trust you when your behavior is consistent. They follow your direction more easily. They believe in your intentions. They feel safer in your presence. Character elevates your influence without needing a higher rank.

Character shapes your legacy. When your career ends, people will remember how you treated them. They will remember your fairness. They will remember your professionalism. They will remember your dignity. Compliance gets the job done. Character determines who you become while doing it.

From Compliance to Character: You follow orders because structure is necessary for safety and consistency. But character determines how you carry out those orders. Two agents can follow the same instruction and produce two very different experiences. The difference lies not in the policy but in the character of the person enforcing it.

Character means staying calm when emotions rise around you. It means using authority with intention instead of impulse. It means speaking with clarity instead of domination. It means treating each person as a human being, regardless of their circumstances.

Character shows whether you act from discipline or from emotion. It shows whether you enforce the law with dignity or with frustration. It shows whether you view your position as a responsibility or as a platform for your ego. Character elevates authority.

Character protects you. When your actions align with your values, you remain steady. You avoid moral injury. You avoid regret. You avoid the internal conflict that comes from acting outside your integrity. Character keeps your conscience clear.

Character builds influence. People trust agents whose actions are consistent. They follow their instructions more willingly. Supervisors notice their professionalism. Colleagues rely on their steadiness.

Character is leadership without needing rank.

Character is the difference between a job and a calling. Compliance fulfills your role. Character defines who you become through that role.

Chapter Nine:

The Compassionate ICE Agent Model

Compassionate leadership in enforcement cannot depend on emotion alone. It requires structure. It requires intention. It requires a framework that keeps you grounded even when the job challenges your patience, your clarity, and your humanity. The Compassionate ICE Agent Model provides that structure. It brings together the qualities that elevate your work and protect your identity.

The first element is awareness. Awareness means paying attention to your internal state and the environment around you. It is recognizing when your tone is becoming short, when your patience is fading, or when your emotions are beginning to lead your decisions. Awareness protects you from reacting impulsively. It also helps you read others more accurately. When you are aware, you understand the difference between fear and aggression, between confusion and resistance.

Awareness gives you the ability to act from clarity instead of instinct.

The second element is patience. Patience is not slow movement. It is controlled movement. It means giving people enough time to understand you. It means pacing your instructions in a way that reduces tension. It means remaining steady when someone is overwhelmed. Patience builds trust. It keeps situations manageable. It is one of the strongest tools an agent can use.

The third element is clarity. Clear communication reduces fear. Clear instructions prevent confusion. Clear explanations bring cooperation. When people understand what is happening, they stop guessing and start listening. Clarity protects your authority because it eliminates unnecessary obstacles. It is a form of compassion that keeps everyone safer.

The fourth element is restraint. Restraint is strength under control. It prevents you from using more force, pressure, or authority than a situation requires. It shows professionalism. It shows discipline. It shows maturity. Restraint preserves dignity for everyone involved. It is the mark of a thoughtful agent, not a reactive one.

The fifth element is dignity. Dignity is the way you hold yourself and the way you treat others. It defines the quality of your authority. When you operate with dignity, you elevate the environment. You reduce fear. You reduce confusion. You prevent unnecessary harm. Dignity creates a respectful atmosphere even when the situation is difficult.

The sixth element is consistency. Consistency builds trust among peers and supervisors. When you respond with steadiness regardless of who is in front of you, people know what to expect. They know you are reliable. They know you are stable. Consistency is leadership expressed through your daily attitude.

The seventh element is reflection. Reflection allows you to grow. It keeps your values alive. It strengthens your self-awareness. It helps you acknowledge mistakes without shame and correct them with maturity. Reflection transforms experience into wisdom. Agents who reflect become wiser, calmer, and more effective.

Together, these elements form the Compassionate ICE Agent. Not a softer agent. Not a naive agent.

A stronger, clearer, more grounded agent who carries authority with purpose and humanity.

Chapter Ten:

Benefits to the Agency and the Nation

Compassion is not only beneficial to you. It benefits the entire agency. It improves the efficiency and safety of operations. It strengthens communication within teams. It reduces internal conflict. It helps agents stay mentally healthy, which improves performance and retention.

Compassion also increases public trust. When the public sees agents who operate with dignity and professionalism, respect for the agency grows. People feel safer engaging with officers. They cooperate more readily. They report information more openly. Compassion strengthens the relationship between the agency and the community it serves.

Compassion reduces unnecessary confrontation. Situations de-escalate more quickly. Emotional tension decreases. Agents remain safer. Communities remain calmer. Compassion supports law enforcement objectives by reducing chaos and confusion.

Compassion improves team morale. When agents treat each other with respect, communication becomes smoother. Trust deepens. Understanding improves. Teams function better. Compassion among colleagues creates a supportive environment that strengthens the unit as a whole.

Compassion strengthens national values. When enforcement is guided by humanity, the nation reflects its ideals more clearly. Laws are upheld without cruelty. Order is maintained without unnecessary harm. Power is used responsibly. This becomes part of the country's moral identity.

The Compassionate ICE Agent is not just a better agent. They are a better representative of the nation's values.

Benefits to the Agency and the Nation: Compassion is not just an individual advantage. It strengthens the entire agency. When agents operate with compassion, communication improves, operational tension decreases, and teamwork becomes more efficient.

The agency benefits because compassionate agents are easier to work with, easier to lead, and easier to trust.

Compassion reduces unnecessary conflict. When agents de-escalate effectively, fewer situations escalate into physical confrontations. This increases safety for agents and civilians. It reduces complaints, investigations, and internal stress. When conflicts decrease, operational flow increases. The agency becomes more efficient and more respected.

Compassion improves public trust. Public trust is not built in press conferences. It is built in daily interactions. When families see that agents treat people with dignity, even during enforcement actions, the agency's reputation strengthens. Communities cooperate more. Reports increase. Fear decreases. Trust with immigrant communities becomes possible.

Compassion strengthens unit morale. Agents who treat each other with respect create a healthier work culture. Communication becomes smoother. Misunderstandings decrease. Support increases. The unit becomes a place where agents feel valued rather than worn down. This reduces turnover and burnout.

Compassion also supports national values. The United States was built on the belief that every human being has dignity. Enforcement guided by compassion reflects those values. It shows that the nation can be strong without being cruel. It shows that order and justice can coexist. It shows that power can be used responsibly.

Compassion contributes to national unity. When people believe the system is fair, they stop viewing enforcement as a threat and begin seeing it as a protective force. Compassion ensures that the work done at the border does not divide the country but reflects its moral identity.

When compassion guides the agency, everyone benefits. Agents grow. Units strengthen. The nation reflects its values. And the badge becomes a symbol not only of authority but of integrity.

Chapter Eleven:

Building a Legacy You Will Be Proud Of

A career in enforcement is not defined by numbers alone. Files are closed. Operations are completed. Statistics are reported and then forgotten. What remains are the moments. The quiet, personal moments that stay in the mind long after the badge is placed in a drawer.

There will be moments when patience replaced frustration. Moments when a calm explanation prevented panic. Moments when dignity was offered in a tense room. Moments when authority was carried with wisdom instead of force. These are the moments that stay. These are the moments that shape the memory of a career.

Years later, when the uniform is no longer worn, those memories return. Not the numbers. Not the reports. The faces return. The voices. The choices made in small, ordinary encounters. Those are the pieces that build a legacy.

A legacy is not created in a single heroic act. It is built quietly, one decision at a time. It grows out of daily conduct. The tone used at a doorway. The patience shown to a frightened parent. The restraint practiced in a heated moment. These small choices reveal who an agent truly is.

Compassion protects that legacy. It keeps the story of a career clean. It ensures that the memories carried into retirement are marked by integrity rather than regret. A career shaped by compassion allows a person to look back with steadiness, not with heaviness.

When compassion guides conduct, it influences more than a single encounter. It shapes the culture around it. Younger agents observe it. Colleagues respond to it. A quiet standard is set, not through speeches, but through behavior. In this way, compassion becomes a form of leadership that continues even after a career ends.

Legacy is not about rank. Titles fade. Positions are filled by others. Legacy is about character. It is about the manner in which authority was carried. It is about the dignity given to others. It is about the respect earned, not demanded.

The future memory of a career is shaped by the way authority was used. There will be recollections of frightened faces and tense rooms. There will be memories of the tone that was chosen, the posture that was carried, the patience that was shown or withheld. Each of those moments leaves a mark on the conscience.

Legacy grows from consistency. It is built through daily behavior, not rare events. Every encounter becomes a small piece of that story. Every decision leaves an impression. Over time, those impressions form the memory of a life in service.

A legacy shaped by compassion brings peace. It allows a person to look back without the weight of regret. It allows conversations with children and grandchildren to carry pride rather than hesitation. It allows the uniform to be remembered as a symbol of integrity.

A legacy built without compassion feels different. It carries questions. It carries moments that replay in the mind. It carries the weight of choices that cannot be undone. That kind of legacy follows a person long after retirement.

Compassion protects the future as much as it shapes

the present. It guards the conscience. It preserves self-respect. It keeps the person behind the badge whole.

Legacy is not measured by how many people were processed or how many operations were completed. It is measured by how those actions were carried out. It is measured by the effect left on the people encountered. It is measured by the dignity preserved in difficult moments.

In the end, the most lasting part of any career is not the authority once held, but the humanity that remained intact while holding it. Compassion ensures that the legacy left behind honors both the role and the person who carried it.

Chapter Twelve:

Past, Present, and Future

Every ICE agent who wears the badge carries a past. That past may include a childhood shaped by discipline, a family that believed in law and order, a parent who wore a uniform, or a moment in life when stability seemed more important than comfort. Some agents came from immigrant families themselves. Some grew up in neighborhoods where the law felt distant. Others were raised in homes where service to country was a sacred duty. Whatever the story, the past is never silent. It sits behind every decision, every tone of voice, every look exchanged at a doorway.

The work of an ICE agent does not exist in isolation. It stands inside a long American story, shaped by the choices of those who came before, the actions of those who serve today, and the legacy that will remain when this generation steps aside. Every era of enforcement carries its own lessons. Some were painful. Some were noble. All of them matter. All of them can guide us, if we are willing to look honestly at where we have been, who we are now, and who we are becoming.

History is not a quiet teacher. It does not whisper its warnings. It speaks clearly to those who are willing to listen. America has walked this road before. Periods of fear, suspicion, and harsh enforcement have appeared many times in our past. Each time, the country believed it was acting in the name of security, order, or survival. Each time, entire communities felt the weight of that fear. Families hid behind curtains. Workers avoided streets. Children grew up with the knowledge that the law could come to their door not as protection, but as a threat.

There were the Chinese exclusion years, when an entire people were labeled unfit for the nation. There were the roundups of the mid-twentieth century, when large sweeps targeted entire communities. There were times when appearance alone was enough to trigger suspicion.

Many who carried out those policies believed they were serving the country faithfully. They believed they were doing their duty. But history did not judge those periods by intention. It judged them by impact. It remembered the fear. It remembered the broken trust. It remembered the families who disappeared from neighborhoods overnight.

After each of those chapters, America looked back and asked itself difficult questions. The country apologized. Laws were revised. Leaders spoke about mistakes. Memorials were built. But apologies do not erase scars. They only prove that the scars were real. The past teaches a simple lesson. Enforcement without compassion never made America stronger. It only made America smaller, colder, and more divided.

Today, the agent stands in the present, where the weight of those lessons is real, even if it is not always spoken. Immigration is no longer an issue confined to distant borders or isolated facilities. It lives in neighborhoods, schools, churches, hospitals, and workplaces. The agent who approaches a door is not just entering a house. He or she is stepping into a web of relationships, fears, hopes, and stories that stretch far beyond that moment.

The present demands balance. It demands strength, but not hardness. It demands clarity, but not cruelty. The weight of cruelty is heavier than most people realize. It does not only affect the migrant. It reshapes the agent as well. It leaves a mark on the heart. It changes the way a person looks at the world. Cruelty may get results quickly. It may create the appearance of efficiency. But it leaves wounds that take years, sometimes generations, to heal.

Cruelty turns communities silent. It teaches people not to trust the badge. It isolates agents from the public they are sworn to serve. It creates an environment where every encounter is tense, every conversation guarded, every uniform feared. In the end, that environment harms everyone, including the agent who must walk through it every day.

Compassion carries weight too, but it is a different kind of weight. It steadies the hand. It clears the mind. It lowers unnecessary tension. It allows families to accept painful outcomes with dignity rather than humiliation. It preserves the moral image of the country, not as a place that abandons its humanity at the first sign of difficulty, but as a nation that holds onto its values even under pressure.

In the present, cruelty may appear efficient, but compassion is what keeps the soul of the country intact. It is what allows an agent to go home at night and feel whole. It is what allows a uniform to be seen not as a threat, but as a symbol of order guided by fairness.

Every agent's personal present is also shaped by the past that brought them to this role. Your past taught you discipline. It shaped your sense of right and wrong. It gave you the reasons you chose to serve. Perhaps you were taught to respect authority. Perhaps you were taught to protect the weak. Perhaps you were taught that a stable society depends on those willing to stand in difficult places. That foundation matters. It is part of who you are. It deserves to be honored.

But the present is where that foundation is tested. It is where policy meets human reality. It is where expectations, pressure, and suffering intersect. It is where your values must become visible through your actions. The present asks for balance. It asks you to carry out your duties with strength, but also with dignity. It asks you to stay steady in moments of conflict. It asks you to protect your humanity while working inside a difficult system.

And then there is the future. The future is not some distant abstraction. It is being built in small moments, one encounter at a time. The future will remember how this generation of agents behaved. It will remember the tone of voice used at doors. It will remember the patience or the impatience. It will remember whether authority was used with restraint or with arrogance.

If cruelty becomes normal, the country of tomorrow will be colder. It will inherit institutions that act with force first and conscience second. And once a nation drifts in that direction, returning to moral clarity becomes difficult. Hardness becomes habit. Suspicion becomes culture. Compassion begins to look like weakness.

But if compassion becomes the guiding principle, the future will be different. It will be a country where agents enforce the law with dignity. Where communities trust those in authority. Where even those who must leave the country carry with them the memory that they were treated as human beings, not as threats. That memory matters more than most people realize. It shapes the way the world sees America. It shapes how children raised here understand justice. It shapes the leaders they will become.

Your own future is tied to those same choices. It depends on what you do each day. It depends on whether you choose compassion when it would be easier to turn away. It depends on whether you act with dignity when frustration rises. It depends on whether you remember the person you promised yourself you would be when you first put on the uniform.

You cannot change your past. You cannot control every outcome in your future. But you can direct your present. That is where your power lives. That is where character is built. That is where compassion becomes visible.

Past, present, and future are not separate ideas. They meet in every decision you make. Your past guides you. Your present tests you. Your future remembers you.

History will not measure this era by the number of arrests or removals. It will measure it by the quality of its humanity during difficult moments. It will ask whether the country defended its laws while honoring the dignity of those who crossed its path. It will ask whether those who wore the badge understood that compassion is strength, not weakness. It will ask whether fear or conscience shaped their decisions.

In every era, America has been defined not by its challenges, but by its response to them. Today, that response lives in the hands of those who serve. The past has shown the cost of cruelty. The present offers the chance to correct the path. And the future will judge whether the courage to lead with compassion was found when it mattered most.

Chapter Thirteenth: Voices of Compassion

This chapter is offered to the circle of people whose lives are shaped, directly or quietly, by immigration enforcement. The badge does not stand alone. It touches homes, classrooms, communities, detention centers, and dinner tables. It touches the lives of agents, their families, the migrants they encounter, and the new recruits who step forward to serve. These messages are written with respect for each part of that circle, and with the belief that compassion gives meaning to every role within it.

To the families of ICE agents, your role is rarely visible, yet it is deeply felt. You see what the public does not see. You notice the tired eyes after long shifts. You hear the quiet that follows difficult days. You feel the emotional weight that enters the home even when no words are spoken. You carry the burdens of a profession you do not perform, simply because you love the person who does.

Your support is not small. It anchors the agent. It

reminds them who they are when the job begins to blur the line between duty and emotion. You are the place where the uniform comes off and the human being returns. In your presence, the badge is no longer the center of the day. In your home, they become a parent again, a spouse again, a son or daughter again. Many agents continue in this work because of the stability you provide.

There are nights when the stress of the job lingers. There are conversations that feel incomplete because some things are too heavy to share. There are days when the tension of the work spills into the home. In those moments, your patience becomes a form of service. Your understanding becomes a shield. Your love becomes the quiet force that keeps the agent steady.

You deserve recognition for that role. You deserve compassion as well. A nation that relies on enforcement must also care for the families who sustain its agents. Support systems, mental health resources, and community understanding should extend to you as much as they extend to those who wear the uniform. You are part of the backbone of this system, even if your contribution is rarely mentioned in public. Your strength deserves respect, and your presence deserves gratitude.

To the trainers and instructors who shape the next generation of agents, your influence reaches far beyond the training room. Recruits may forget policy numbers and procedural codes, but they will remember you. They will remember the tone you used, the presence you carried, and the values you demonstrated when they were still forming their professional identity.

You are not only teaching tactics or procedures. You are shaping instincts. You are building habits of judgment. You are forming the inner compass that agents will rely on when the field places them in complex and emotional situations. The culture they create tomorrow begins with the culture you build today.

Every instruction becomes part of their foundation. The way you speak to them becomes the way they speak to others. The way you handle tension becomes the way they handle conflict. You have the opportunity to create agents who are strong without being harsh, firm without being cruel, confident without arrogance, and prepared without losing their humanity.

Teach them that restraint is a form of control. Teach them that patience often leads to cooperation. Teach them that clarity prevents conflict. Teach them that dignity is not an extra step but the foundation of professional conduct. When recruits see compassion modeled by their instructors, they carry it into the field as part of their identity, not as an afterthought.

Agents remember the instructor who spoke with fairness. They remember the one who carried calm into tense simulations. They remember the one who said that strength and kindness are not enemies. Through them, your influence extends into homes, communities, and moments of great vulnerability. You are not only preparing them for a job. You are shaping the moral climate of the institution.

To the new recruits entering this profession, the path ahead will demand more than physical readiness or procedural knowledge. It will demand clarity of judgment, emotional strength, and a steady sense of humanity. You will encounter people at some of the most difficult moments of their lives. You will stand in doorways where fear lives. You will carry authority that must be used with care.

At the beginning of this journey, remember one simple truth. The badge does not define you. Your character does. The uniform gives you authority, but your humanity gives that authority meaning. Without character, the badge is only metal and cloth. With character, it becomes a symbol of justice.

You will face moments where frustration rises. You will meet people who are angry, frightened, or confused. In those moments, the way you carry yourself will shape the entire interaction. A calm voice can prevent panic. A patient posture can reduce resistance. A clear explanation can restore order.

This career will change you. Let it change you in strength, not hardness. Let it deepen your understanding rather than dull your compassion. The strongest agents are not those who feel the least. They are the ones who remain steady and human through difficult work. Serve with pride, but also with balance. The country needs agents who are disciplined and deeply humane at the same time.

To the migrants who arrived in the United States searching for safety, dignity, or opportunity, your worth is not defined by your immigration status. Your humanity is not erased by a document, a case number, or a legal decision. Many of you left homes, families, and familiar streets because survival required it. Many of you carried hope across borders and through hardship. That courage is real, and it deserves recognition.

You deserve to be treated with fairness. You deserve clarity about your situation. You deserve dignity, regardless of the outcome of your case. Enforcement does not erase your value as a person. A system may judge your legal standing, but it cannot measure your worth as a human being.

This country is built on laws, but it is also built on people. People who once arrived as strangers. People who once carried uncertainty in their hearts. Many of them now stand as citizens, leaders, neighbors, and friends. The story of migration is woven into the very fabric of this nation.

You are more than statistics. You are more than headlines. You are individuals with histories, families, and dreams. If your path continues here, may it lead to stability. If your path leads elsewhere, may you carry with you the memory that dignity was present even in difficult moments. Your story does not end at a border, and your humanity does not end with a decision.

These voices form a circle around the badge. Families who support it. Trainers who shape it. Recruits who inherit it. Migrants who encounter it. And those who depart under its authority. When compassion lives within that circle, the nation remains closer to the ideals it claims.

May the law be carried with dignity. May authority remain guided by humanity. And may compassion continue to shape the American experience for all who walk within it.

This page intentionally left blank for your reading reflection

As you leave

To those who leave the United States through deportation, remember your departure does not erase your dignity. It does not diminish your worth. It does not define your entire story. You came seeking safety or opportunity. You worked hard, loved deeply, and tried to build a stable life for yourself and families. Your efforts were real, even if your path was interrupted.

As you leave, please remember that America is a nation that seeks to forgive and to grow. Whatever tensions existed, whatever mistakes were made on any side, carry with you the memory that this country is capable of fairness, capable of compassion, and capable of recognizing your humanity. Forgive our aggressions as we aggressed against you. Forgive the moments when fear overshadowed dignity. Forgive the times when policy overwhelmed understanding.

Your departure is not a closing door. Carry with you the hope that justice can evolve. Carry the knowledge that many Americans wish you well. Carry the truth that your life still holds meaning and possibility beyond this journey. Though the path leads away from America for now, it does not close the chapters of your strength, your courage, or your future.

A nation is judged not only by how it welcomes people but also by how it lets them go. May you leave with dignity. May you leave knowing that your humanity remains intact. May you leave believing that forgiveness and compassion can heal what fear once divided.

My Final Thoughts

As I return to the reason I began this journey with you. I wanted us to cherish and protect the American experience from quietly losing its soul. I wanted to speak to the men and women who wear the ICE badge, not as critics or opponents, but as compassionate human beings who deserve clarity, and dignity in the work they do.

I wanted to speak to the people who fear them, to remind them that compassion is still possible even in difficult moments. And I wanted to speak to the country itself, to remind us that who we become depends on how we treat one another.

To the ICE agents who serve this nation, this book is a message of respect and gratitude to your dedication. Your work is demanding. It pulls you into situations most Americans will never witness.

You carry stress that is rarely acknowledged and responsibilities that are often misunderstood. But even in this difficult work, you still have a choice in how you serve. You can enforce the law with clarity and dignity. You can protect the country without breaking the spirit of those you encounter. You can walk away from every shift knowing you acted with both firmness and humanity. Compassion will not weaken your authority. It will strengthen your character.

To ICE leadership, your role shapes the culture of the entire agency. Remember, leadership always sets the tone. The tone you set becomes the behavior your agents follow. When you model fairness, agents serve with fairness. When you uphold dignity, agents reflects that dignity. When you recognize the human cost of enforcement, you help your teams carry their burdens without losing themselves. You have the opportunity to guide this agency toward a future where compassion is not an exception but an expectation.

To the undocumented you tasted the generosity of America. Even if the law requires you to leave, may you carry the memory that this nation is capable of fairness. Forgive our moments of fear. Forgive the times we failed to see your humanity. Your courage remains yours. Your dignity remains yours.

To the American people, our strength as a nation has always come from compassion. Laws matter, but the way we enforce them matters just as much. We cannot claim moral leadership while abandoning humanity. We cannot build unity while deepening fear. We cannot protect America by losing the very values that made it a place worth protecting.

I wrote this book to remind us that ICE agents can honor both the law and the human beings who stand before them. It is about guiding leaders to create a culture where dignity is the standard and compassion is a sign of strength.

If these pages help even one agent act with more humanity, even one leader rethink their approach, even one migrant leave with dignity, or even one American understand the importance of compassion in enforcement, then this work has served its purpose.

America is at its best when it holds its power with humility and its authority with care. My hope is that this book moves us one step closer to that promise.

To the ICE Agents, thank you for your service.

This page intentionally left blank for your reading reflection

10-Day Reflection Exercise

10-Day Reflection

Exercise for ICE Agents

Rule

For the next ten days, set aside **15 quiet minutes at the end of each shift** to reflect on your conduct, tone, and decisions throughout the day.

Do not judge yourself harshly. Do not justify your actions either. Simply observe, record, and become aware.

The purpose of this exercise is **self-awareness.**

Compassion begins with awareness.
Awareness begins with honest reflection.
Each day, note how many times you were:

- Kind
- Considerate
- Courteous
- Patient
- Clear in your communication

- Respectful under pressure

Also note any moment where you felt tension, frustration, or regret.

Daily Reflection Form – Day 1

Day: __________________ Date: ________________

Shift Type (field, office, transport, etc.): ______

1. Encounters Today

Approximate number of people you interacted with: _______

2. Compassion Check

How many times today were you:

- Kind: _______
- Considerate: _______
- Courteous: _______
- Patient: _______
- Clear in your communication: _______
- Respectful under pressure: _______

3. One Positive Moment

Describe one moment where you handled a situation with dignity or compassion:

---

4. One Challenging Moment

Describe a moment that felt tense, rushed, or emotionally difficult:

---

5. Self-Awareness Question

In that challenging moment, how did you carry your authority?

☐ Calm and steady

☐ Neutral and procedural

☐ Rushed or tense

☐ Frustrated

☐ Other: ____________________

6. What Could Have Been Done Differently

Without blaming yourself, note one small thing you could adjust next time:

____

____

7. Emotional State at End of Shift

How do you feel right now?

☐ Clear and steady
☐ Tired but calm
☐ Mentally drained
☐ Frustrated
☐ Heavy or uneasy
☐ Other: ____________________

8. One Intention for Tomorrow

Write one simple intention for the next shift:

Examples:

- "Speak more slowly."
- "Explain procedures more clearly."
- "Stay calm when tension rises."

Your intention:

Daily Reflection Form – Day 2

Day: ________________ Date: ______________

Shift Type (field, office, transport, etc.): _____

1. Encounters Today

Approximate number of people you interacted with: ______

2. Compassion Check

How many times today were you:

- Kind: ______
- Considerate: ______
- Courteous: ______
- Patient: ______
- Clear in your communication: ______
- Respectful under pressure: ______

3. One Positive Moment

Describe one moment where you handled a situation with dignity or compassion:

____

____

____

4. One Challenging Moment

Describe a moment that felt tense, rushed, or emotionally difficult:

____

____

____

5. Self-Awareness Question

In that challenging moment, how did you carry your authority?

☐ Calm and steady
☐ Neutral and procedural
☐ Rushed or tense
☐ Frustrated
☐ Other: ____________________

6. What Could Have Been Done Differently

Without blaming yourself, note one small thing you could adjust next time:

____

____

7. Emotional State at End of Shift

How do you feel right now?

☐ Clear and steady
☐ Tired but calm
☐ Mentally drained
☐ Frustrated
☐ Heavy or uneasy
☐ Other: ____________________

8. One Intention for Tomorrow

Write one simple intention for the next shift:

Examples:

- "Speak more slowly."
- "Explain procedures more clearly."
- "Stay calm when tension rises."

Your intention:

Daily Reflection Form – Day 3

Day: __________________ Date: ________________

Shift Type (field, office, transport, etc.): ______

1. Encounters Today

Approximate number of people you interacted with: _______

2. Compassion Check

How many times today were you:

- Kind: _______
- Considerate: _______
- Courteous: _______
- Patient: _______
- Clear in your communication: _______
- Respectful under pressure: _______

3. One Positive Moment

Describe one moment where you handled a situation with dignity or compassion:

4. One Challenging Moment

Describe a moment that felt tense, rushed, or emotionally difficult:

5. Self-Awareness Question

In that challenging moment, how did you carry your authority?

☐ Calm and steady

☐ Neutral and procedural

☐ Rushed or tense

☐ Frustrated

☐ Other: ____________________

6. What Could Have Been Done Differently

Without blaming yourself, note one small thing you could adjust next time:

____

____

7. Emotional State at End of Shift

How do you feel right now?

☐ Clear and steady
☐ Tired but calm
☐ Mentally drained
☐ Frustrated
☐ Heavy or uneasy
☐ Other: ____________________

8. One Intention for Tomorrow

Write one simple intention for the next shift:

Examples:

- "Speak more slowly."
- "Explain procedures more clearly."
- "Stay calm when tension rises."

Your intention:

Daily Reflection Form – Day 4

Day: ________________ Date: ______________

Shift Type (field, office, transport, etc.): _____

1. Encounters Today

Approximate number of people you interacted with: _______

2. Compassion Check

How many times today were you:

- Kind: _______
- Considerate: _______
- Courteous: _______
- Patient: _______
- Clear in your communication: _______
- Respectful under pressure: _______

3. One Positive Moment

Describe one moment where you handled a situation with dignity or compassion:

---

4. One Challenging Moment

Describe a moment that felt tense, rushed, or emotionally difficult:

---

5. Self-Awareness Question

In that challenging moment, how did you carry your authority?

☐ Calm and steady
☐ Neutral and procedural
☐ Rushed or tense
☐ Frustrated
☐ Other: ____________________

6. What Could Have Been Done Differently

Without blaming yourself, note one small thing you could adjust next time:

____

____

7. Emotional State at End of Shift

How do you feel right now?

☐ Clear and steady
☐ Tired but calm
☐ Mentally drained
☐ Frustrated
☐ Heavy or uneasy
☐ Other: ____________________

8. One Intention for Tomorrow

Write one simple intention for the next shift:

Examples:

- "Speak more slowly."
- "Explain procedures more clearly."
- "Stay calm when tension rises."

Your intention:

Daily Reflection Form – Day 5

Day: ________________ Date: ______________

Shift Type (field, office, transport, etc.): _____

1. Encounters Today

Approximate number of people you interacted with: ______

2. Compassion Check

How many times today were you:

- Kind: ______
- Considerate: ______
- Courteous: ______
- Patient: ______
- Clear in your communication: ______
- Respectful under pressure: ______

3. One Positive Moment

Describe one moment where you handled a situation with dignity or compassion:

____

____

____

4. One Challenging Moment

Describe a moment that felt tense, rushed, or emotionally difficult:

____

____

____

5. Self-Awareness Question

In that challenging moment, how did you carry your authority?

☐ Calm and steady
☐ Neutral and procedural
☐ Rushed or tense
☐ Frustrated
☐ Other: ____________________

6. What Could Have Been Done Differently

Without blaming yourself, note one small thing you could adjust next time:

____

____

7. Emotional State at End of Shift

How do you feel right now?

☐ Clear and steady
☐ Tired but calm
☐ Mentally drained
☐ Frustrated
☐ Heavy or uneasy
☐ Other: ____________________

8. One Intention for Tomorrow

Write one simple intention for the next shift:

Examples:

- "Speak more slowly."
- "Explain procedures more clearly."
- "Stay calm when tension rises."

Your intention:

Daily Reflection Form – Day 6

Day: ________________ Date: ______________

Shift Type (field, office, transport, etc.): _____

1. Encounters Today

Approximate number of people you interacted with: ______

2. Compassion Check

How many times today were you:

- Kind: ______
- Considerate: ______
- Courteous: ______
- Patient: ______
- Clear in your communication: ______
- Respectful under pressure: ______

3. One Positive Moment

Describe one moment where you handled a situation with dignity or compassion:

---

4. One Challenging Moment

Describe a moment that felt tense, rushed, or emotionally difficult:

---

5. Self-Awareness Question

In that challenging moment, how did you carry your authority?

☐ Calm and steady
☐ Neutral and procedural
☐ Rushed or tense
☐ Frustrated
☐ Other: ____________________

6. What Could Have Been Done Differently

Without blaming yourself, note one small thing you could adjust next time:

____

____

7. Emotional State at End of Shift

How do you feel right now?

☐ Clear and steady
☐ Tired but calm
☐ Mentally drained
☐ Frustrated
☐ Heavy or uneasy
☐ Other: ____________________

8. One Intention for Tomorrow

Write one simple intention for the next shift:

Examples:

- "Speak more slowly."
- "Explain procedures more clearly."
- "Stay calm when tension rises."

Your intention:

Daily Reflection Form – Day 7

Day: ________________ Date: ______________

Shift Type (field, office, transport, etc.): _____

1. Encounters Today

Approximate number of people you interacted with: ______

2. Compassion Check

How many times today were you:

- Kind: ______
- Considerate: ______
- Courteous: ______
- Patient: ______
- Clear in your communication: ______
- Respectful under pressure: ______

3. One Positive Moment

Describe one moment where you handled a situation with dignity or compassion:

4. One Challenging Moment

Describe a moment that felt tense, rushed, or emotionally difficult:

5. Self-Awareness Question

In that challenging moment, how did you carry your authority?

☐ Calm and steady
☐ Neutral and procedural
☐ Rushed or tense
☐ Frustrated
☐ Other: ____________________

6. What Could Have Been Done Differently

Without blaming yourself, note one small thing you could adjust next time:

____

____

7. Emotional State at End of Shift

How do you feel right now?

☐ Clear and steady
☐ Tired but calm
☐ Mentally drained
☐ Frustrated
☐ Heavy or uneasy
☐ Other: ____________________

8. One Intention for Tomorrow

Write one simple intention for the next shift:

Examples:

- "Speak more slowly."
- "Explain procedures more clearly."
- "Stay calm when tension rises."

Your intention:

Daily Reflection Form – Day 8

Day: ____________________ Date: ________________

Shift Type (field, office, transport, etc.): ______

1. Encounters Today

Approximate number of people you interacted with: _______

2. Compassion Check

How many times today were you:

- Kind: _______
- Considerate: _______
- Courteous: _______
- Patient: _______
- Clear in your communication: _______
- Respectful under pressure: _______

3. One Positive Moment

Describe one moment where you handled a situation with dignity or compassion:

____

____

____

4. One Challenging Moment

Describe a moment that felt tense, rushed, or emotionally difficult:

____

____

____

5. Self-Awareness Question

In that challenging moment, how did you carry your authority?

☐ Calm and steady
☐ Neutral and procedural
☐ Rushed or tense
☐ Frustrated
☐ Other: ____________________

6. What Could Have Been Done Differently

Without blaming yourself, note one small thing you could adjust next time:

____

____

7. Emotional State at End of Shift

How do you feel right now?

☐ Clear and steady
☐ Tired but calm
☐ Mentally drained
☐ Frustrated
☐ Heavy or uneasy
☐ Other: ___________________

8. One Intention for Tomorrow

Write one simple intention for the next shift:

Examples:

- "Speak more slowly."
- "Explain procedures more clearly."
- "Stay calm when tension rises."

Your intention:

Daily Reflection Form – Day 9

Day: ________________ Date: ______________

Shift Type (field, office, transport, etc.): _____

1. Encounters Today

Approximate number of people you interacted with: ______

2. Compassion Check

How many times today were you:

- Kind: ______
- Considerate: ______
- Courteous: ______
- Patient: ______
- Clear in your communication: ______
- Respectful under pressure: ______

3. One Positive Moment

Describe one moment where you handled a situation with dignity or compassion:

4. One Challenging Moment

Describe a moment that felt tense, rushed, or emotionally difficult:

5. Self-Awareness Question

In that challenging moment, how did you carry your authority?

☐ Calm and steady
☐ Neutral and procedural
☐ Rushed or tense
☐ Frustrated
☐ Other: ____________________

6. What Could Have Been Done Differently

Without blaming yourself, note one small thing you could adjust next time:

____

____

7. Emotional State at End of Shift

How do you feel right now?

☐ Clear and steady
☐ Tired but calm
☐ Mentally drained
☐ Frustrated
☐ Heavy or uneasy
☐ Other: ____________________

8. One Intention for Tomorrow

Write one simple intention for the next shift:

Examples:

- "Speak more slowly."
- "Explain procedures more clearly."
- "Stay calm when tension rises."

Your intention:

Daily Reflection Form – Day 10

Day: _________________ Date: _______________

Shift Type (field, office, transport, etc.): _____

1. Encounters Today

Approximate number of people you interacted with: _______

2. Compassion Check

How many times today were you:

- Kind: _______
- Considerate: _______
- Courteous: _______
- Patient: _______
- Clear in your communication: _______
- Respectful under pressure: _______

3. One Positive Moment

Describe one moment where you handled a situation with dignity or compassion:

____

____

____

4. One Challenging Moment

Describe a moment that felt tense, rushed, or emotionally difficult:

____

____

____

5. Self-Awareness Question

In that challenging moment, how did you carry your authority?

☐ Calm and steady
☐ Neutral and procedural
☐ Rushed or tense
☐ Frustrated
☐ Other: ____________________

6. What Could Have Been Done Differently

Without blaming yourself, note one small thing you could adjust next time:

____

____

7. Emotional State at End of Shift

How do you feel right now?

☐ Clear and steady
☐ Tired but calm
☐ Mentally drained
☐ Frustrated
☐ Heavy or uneasy
☐ Other: ____________________

8. One Intention for Tomorrow

Write one simple intention for the next shift:

Examples:

- "Speak more slowly."
- "Explain procedures more clearly."
- "Stay calm when tension rises."

Your intention:

End of Day 10 – Final Reflection

After completing all ten days, take one longer reflection.

1. What patterns did you notice in your behavior?

___

___

___

2. Did compassion make your work easier or harder?

___

___

___

3. What one habit would you like to carry forward?

___

___

___

4. What kind of legacy do you want to build in this profession?

This page intentionally left blank for your reading reflection

About Dr. Abraham Khoureis, Ph.D.

Dr. Abraham Khoureis, Ph.D., was named the Apostle of Compassionate Leadership by his colleagues and leadership professional inner circle. A multi-talented thought leader and partner, author, an award-winning mentor, and advocate for compassionate leadership. He is an adjunct professor who specializes in teaching graduate-level courses in business and management, blending academic theory with real-world business practices.

Dr. Khoureis is also a small business owner and holds numerous state certifications and professional designations showcasing his multidisciplinary expertise.

He is the Creator of the Compassionate Leadership Model and Pyramid, which emphasizes leadership built on self-awareness, mindfulness, and commitment to serving others without expectation of return.

Moreover, Dr. Khoureis developed the Disability Learning Attainment Model, a framework designed to empower individuals with disabilities through inclusive education, skill-building, and leadership development. Through his writing, he advocates and advances positive societal change. His work champions and empowers inclusivity, accessibility, and ethical practices in both education and leadership. He has been published on *Forbes.com*, *Newsweek.com*, and the distinguished *Leader to Leader Journal*. He was recognized as LinkedIn's Top Leadership and Management Voice, and Thinkers 360's Top 50 Voices.

Dr. Abe's contributions extend to his writings, professional leadership development initiatives, and thought leadership, making him a respected emerging leader in the fields of compassionate leadership, organizational behavior, and human development.

Easily accessible at: DrAbeKhoureis.com

AuthorDrAbeKhoureis.com

Social Media: @DrAbeKhoureis

DrAbeBooks.com

For his latest published work, visit Amazon.com and search for Dr. Abraham Khoureis, Ph.D.

Other Books by Dr. Abraham Khoureis, Ph.D.

The Balance In Between: Finding the Balance Between Emotional Intelligence and Emotional Stupidity. ISBN: 979-8-9895211-2-8

Decoding Microaggressions for Leaders and Beyond: Understanding Microaggressions Face-to-Face. ISBN: 979-8-9895211-4-2

Hollywood Dream: How To Make It In Tinseltown. ISBN: 979-8-9895211-7-3

Protect Your Business: Stay Informed, Stay Ahead. ISBN: 978-1-966837-09-1

Revealing the Seven Secrets to Exceptional Mentorship. ISBN: 978-1-966837-00-8

SELF: Introducing The Self Rotating Model. ISBN: 979-8-9895211-5-9

The Compassionate Leadership Model and Pyramid. ISBN: 979-8-9895211-0-4

This page intentionally left blank for your reading reflection

www.ingramcontent.com/pod-product-compliance
Lightning Source LLC
Chambersburg PA
CBHW060905280326
41934CB00007B/1191

* 9 7 8 1 9 6 6 8 3 7 4 6 6 *